I0500806

Self-Injury <u>Disorder</u>

Now- can we get a little help over here!

Table of Contents located on page 21

Dedicated to my children~

My daughter for fighting this on her own with strength and ethics, and her brother for standing by her and loving her the whole way. And, of course, to you- the ones looking for or trying to – *help.*

Self-injury—

those are hard words to even say. Some people say cutting- I think that might be easier- less truth. Of course cutting isn't the only form of self-injury. The definition is far and wide and to me encompasses so much more than we allow for- where does self-injury end? But we are dealing with a new concept for many people and I just want to get some understanding out there. It's so dark and secretive that there is little help available. Most professional's only guess at the origins and the meaning and many openly show disgust. I will try to take you into a world you never expected to enter, I hope to help you understand, maybe offer some guidance - but mostly hope. Can you imagine that I am saying- its really not as bad as you are thinking, it's not near as horrific or disgusting as many of you think.

Ready? I'm not a writer and I have no clue how to make this flow- but for a few years I have known I have to get this out there and try to help this situation-- so Ready? Take a deep breath and let's try to get through this. I'll help you the best I can. If you are a 'cutter', someone who loves one or a professional hoping to help- my hope is to offer you something here. I think the best way I can communicate with you is to talk to you like you are my friend-- so I will try to write this in such a way - at least that's how I am going to start.

If you are wondering if your loved one is a cutter, then probably – 'yes'. Don't' deny it don't hide from it- let's just step right into this right now, and get going on the way to helping.

I learned my incredibly talented and beautiful daughter was cutting her beautiful arms the summer she was 14. I was leaving for work, and every morning I would stop in and say good-bye and leave the phone with her. She wore long sleeves but you know kids and styles? Her sleeve was pushed up and I saw a cut- sort of like a deep cat scratch, but we didn't have cats. She called me every day when she woke up and I asked that day- what happened to her arms-- silence--- I asked did she do that to herself--- silence-- I felt like I was going to vomit and with no understanding of what was happening. I told her I was on my way home. She was crying - I was crying and I went home. I'm not even sure if I told my boss. There we sat on her bed crying- neither of us understanding- that's right-

Neither of us understood.

The only person she wanted to tell was her older brother - a 17-year-old boy. He took it better than you think anyone would.

It's a lot to take in initially but her brother did well. We sat down - the three of us and talked-- a very short talk at first- just to get it out there. He didn't understand any more than either of us did. But there we were - together. That was the big thing.

We were there- unconditionally - a family.

It's self-injury-- you can say it, quietly at first... let the words fall from your mouth and touch the silence around your ears. A sinking feeling falls around you and so many unpleasant feelings surround you, it's hard to breathe. Self-injury- it sounds awful- I know. And someone you love and adore feels compelled to hurt him or herself. Even worse- all this and you didn't see it; you didn't recognize warnings and you didn't stop it. This happened right here, right under your nose, right in your safe home. Where did you go wrong? Yes, that's it. Where could you have prevented it- why didn't you know about it why didn't you stop it? You did so much right you tried so hard - I know. And you still failed her. How awful. You want to run from it, pretend it isn't real. But please don't. First thing we have to do--- make sure you know this isn't about you-- it's not yours. Stop whining and crying and dealing with your 'me' stuff. This is all about someone you love and you have to step past yesterday and into 'right now' and let go of all your wondering and worrying and thoughts of yourself and where you went wrong and where you failed them and how hard you tried and how you didn't know and how it isn't fair and—well- All that stuff. You will need a moment here pretty soon. You need to take a personal moment, step aside and do whatever it is you need to do—scream, cry, yell, fall down sobbing onto the ground, feel sorry for yourself -

whatever--- away from everyone. Get it over with - because you have to get back here and help make this right. *I had to do this- I never crashed like I did with this. I fell to the ground sobbing and I am a person who rarely cries. I cannot even begin to tell you what I felt-- lost, hurt, alone, scared, failed, worthless, helpless.... everything bad. But I stood back up... because what else am I going to do? Deep breath--- and we have to make it better. Here is my baby - injuring herself- on purpose. My baby I spend so much time with and love so much-- where did I fail her? Way too many thoughts to even get through them all.*

And here you are with Swirling, painful, badness.

First thing if you begged cried or demanded they stop-- suck it up- you are going to have to retract that. Yes, you are. This is bigger than what you see so don't make it worse. See -- the best I can explain it-- self-injury is a release, like crying-- this is how they have found to release their pain and anguish-- if you stop them from using the only means they know helps them relieve pain-- you have to know that it may become too much, and then what?

First thing I said to her was promise me you will never do this again... both of us crying - she promised... but why, how, what, was going on?! But she agreed to never do it again. I felt better. Then I went to do research-- so little and so mixed up... but I read over and over that this is their release for all the pain inside... and if there is no release there is eventually something very bad... maybe suicide. Oh my, I couldn't have that-- so I took a deep breath and did something you never think you will do... I took my precious daughter aside and talked to her about all of this-- and told her, I do not want you to hurt yourself, I will be here for you as much as I possibly can, I will find anyway possible to help make this better and keep it from happening. We will try different things and if you ever need me get me and I mean anytime-- wake me, call me-- get me. But - if you cannot stand it any more-- then I understand-- be very careful, be safe, try to take it easy. That was a sickening thing to say, but I couldn't risk something worse. We went to the store and bought first aid products for her to keep. This way if she did it she could keep it medicated and avoid further problems. And she wouldn't have to go to me and say she did it- to get medication-- she felt like such a failure already. Safety was most important. I told her to be careful for major arteries and told her, If she cut herself and the bleeding didn't stop to call 911 then call me and apply pressure and remain as calm as possible. That's another one of those 'Yuck' moments.

Then to get help, to get understanding, to figure it out and work on stopping it. I read everything I could find and it was such a mess of stupidity and guesswork that - we were on our own. Books, psychiatrist, counselors, and hospitals--- they all failed us-- and actually made it worse for her. My family couldn't be told. They wouldn't handle it well and my daughter didn't want them to know. So we started with **psychiatrists- they were expensive - even with insurance, but instantly, without conversation or**

consideration they wanted her on drugs. There she was 14 and they wanted her on drugs without even speaking to her. Their reasoning was 'well- it's self-injury so she must be really messed up'.

We tried several 'counselors' who had their own preset ideas of the underlying issues and how to treat them without ever talking to us. I talked to preachers who find solution in prayer- and I already did that, all day every day at this point. I talked to a friend who was a police counselor and he had some reasonable advice but it was not therapy or counseling – it was mostly just telling me to stop being upset and deal with it, but he couldn't be of any ongoing treatment plan. I did internet searches and read any book I could find. I read blogs by cutters, and tried online help, but really no matter how hard I tried -I simply could not find anyone who was of any real *help!*

So there- no hope for help?

Yes, you will find yourself standing in a lost place feeling very alone. Most do not understand and don't want to try.

That was several years ago but still I find there is no help and still there is very little understanding. *That's where we started though...*

Here's the hardest and the easiest thing you need to know... there is no secret cure, but you can handle it.

So on our own we had to figure out something because living this way was too hard. The first thing you want to do is understand this. Well, if they don't know why they do it- they surely cannot explain it to you so there's no need to harass them and nag them and push them for a reason. They most likely have no way to explain. Here's all I can explain—for whatever reason a person who resorts to self-injury does not know how to release their pain. Some accepted ways of releasing bad feelings are drinking, smoking, fighting, hitting things, sex, drugs, over exercise, yelling, driving fast and eating too much or eating disorders. Yes, I said accepted ways... society accepts these things and looks on self-injury with disgust. All these things and more are things we accept and show sympathy and understanding for – and there is help for these things. Self-injury is still taboo and hidden in the darkest places of society. We can't talk about it so how can we do anything to figure it out or help with it?

I do not understand why it's accepted and empathized with if someone has a drug problem or an eating disorder but self-

injury is considered so awful. Tell me—
aren't all these things a form of self-
injury? Yes, they are. So why is this so
hard for society to accept and deal with?
I guess that's my biggest point of anger—
the disgust and in turn the lack of help.
Most people would rather not see it and
not deal with it... and just make it go
away. The thing is it won't just go away.
And why is it better to have done drugs
than this? **It's not**.
So the first thing you have to do is
accept it. It is happening- it's real. Then
you need to realize- there is very little
help and very little understanding. If you
are supporting someone who suffers from
self-injury understand there are no easy
answers and it's a process. It's not a
'cure and move on' kind of thing. It's
always going to be there and it may always
be a battle somewhere in their mind.
They cannot just be cured and if you
assume they can be then you will leave

them in a place of vulnerability and continued misunderstanding. You will have to just get through it and consider every day without self-injury a huge win.. and on days when they slip—it's just a day they slipped-NOT A FAILURE!—just one day of many. And the next day is a day to move forward and try again. They may make it a day then a week then a month then maybe a few months, but know that it's a struggle on some of those days and on some of those days they will slip—but pick it up right after. Let them know how proud you are of them for making it when they do and that you never consider it a failure on bad days... and you are just as dedicated and ready to keep working at it. It is never a failure. They are just struggling with little help, and almost no understanding of how they suffer. They may feel horrible and stupid and like a freak. They are not- make sure they know they are not any of those things, and please try to help them understand you feel inadequate yourself for not knowing what to do or why this happens.

I'm trying, but I am not a writer. Hope you can follow this, I hope it helps some.

Everyone who tries to understand will have his or her own ideas of what causes self-injury. I say it's just another form of the many ways we self-injure. It's more direct and more visible than other forms but really what extreme behavior is not self-injury? The thing about 'cutting' is you can see it- it's right there—and then the scars are real to see. You cannot hide from it as easily as other things.

Unconditional love-
that will help you through.

Once you accept it and deal with it—you see it everywhere and people will be drawn to you just to speak to someone who isn't scared or disgusted. Someone they can talk to about it without feeling like a freak. *After I learned my daughter was a 'cutter' so many people just told me about their problems. It was amazing.* So many kids are self-injurers. Their parents sometimes know, sometimes they don't know. There are warning signs and even psychiatrists' don't see them and don't warn us.

Any form of self-injury should be dealt with immediately. I'm talking about hitting walls, scratching themselves, pulling their hair, hitting themselves, drastic hair cuts, tattoos and piercings-- self-injury—is simply injuring themselves. Anything—it's a warning—pay attention.

I don't know if you can stop it if you catch it early- but I would suggest you recognize it and start dealing with it. Look for the warnings and try to make it better.

Look for the cover-ups----

Long sleeves, pants and just keeping flesh covered when they didn't before. Scratches, cuts, burns—don't ignore them. Broken razors, broken glass, knives, any sharp objects, lighters, matches and candles—can all be used for self-injury... if it looks odd—pay attention.. If it can be used to self injure—it's okay to ask.

You can talk to your loved one about it. Talking to them about it won't make them do it if they are not. Don't accuse them-- talk to them. You can ask if they know what self-injury is and open a conversation with them. Let them know you are aware it is a real issue for many people today- let them know you understand it is not well known and does not get much help, let them know you do not judge people who deal with this. Try to be open with them.

Be a safe person for them to talk to about this or anything.

They are so alone and so confused and hurting so bad—be strong- be caring and help. Deal with your own drama separately- don't make this about you or how hard it is on you. They really don't need the added pressure of your hurt and your pain. They need your help and they need to have a safe place to get better.

 Don't judge what they are dealing with. Don't make it worse.

Okay, I don't want to just ramble here but I never expected to ever try to write a book, so having any clue how to write one or figure out how to write one – well, its just not ever been a thought. I just know there has to be some understanding of this somehow.

I thought if I try to separate it into parts- maybe that will help. Like a book should be, so wrong place but here are

the contents:

So –
UNDERSTANDING

That may be too hard for some of you. The thing is I cannot understand why anyone would smoke or need to drink- because I don't have that need. But we have to step into a different place in our mind and at least understand some very basic things:

First, **it's real.**
I hear a lot of people say self-injury is just being done for attention. I want to spew profanity at that stupidity- really?! For attention? You would inflict pain and long-term scars on your body simply for attention? Its self-injury- no matter why you think it's happening you still need to deal with it. I think some people can deal with it easier if they believe it is done for attention. That it somehow makes it easier to put into a category and be angry

at them. Please don't do that, please don't go there. Let's just try to deal with this on a realistic level. And if you think they are doing it for attention- well, it's still self-injury and it still needs help so you are still in the same spot – you just think you understand, "why". You can empathize, you can sympathize, you can pick it apart and you can ignore it- but to truly internally deeply understand it- well, unless you feel it- I don't think you can understand how it feels.

Next – **it's how someone you love handles bad feelings.** Try this- how bad do you have to feel to self injure!? Pretty bad I would guess. So accept that no matter how good you think their life is or how hard you try to make it right or what it does to you—this person hurts so bad that they feel better by inflicting injury onto themselves. Whatever you think they should feel doesn't matter –what matters is- that's how bad they feel. I don't know how they discover self-injury makes it feel better. Probably accidentally- scratching their fists when they are angry, punching a wall, picking nails until they bleed? Or maybe it's something they are drawn to do? The thing is – that doesn't matter so much- what matters is – you need to understand they hurt very badly and this make them feel better, so they do it. Usually as a last resort when they cannot take any more they resort to self inflicted injury. Whatever you do- probably doesn't work for them or they would do it. This is what they have found that works to relieve their pain and bad stuff. It works so they do it. They will do it over and over. When they do it then they will feel worse about themselves that they 'failed' so then they crash harder and do it more. Maybe something like bingeing when you fail at your efforts to lose weight?

It's not a fad-

Ignoring it won't make it go away. You can hide from it and leave them to handle it all on their own- but it's not going away. So if it's so hard for you to handle- that you want to ignore it- please think what they must be dealing with – it's too alone and too painful already. And if people they love refuse to deal with it, then that makes it so much worse. Please deal with it. Please help them. Please look at it and don't ignore it. Please look at it with love and understand-- they have enough to deal with, so don't make it worse by being so put off by it that you ignore it and pretend it's just going to go away.

Many addictive behaviors are actually self-injury-

Overeating, smoking, drinking, extreme exercise, too much sex, drugs, eating disorders—every problem that we allow so much empathy and understanding and help for—aren't they all injury to the body and/or mind and doesn't that make it all self-injury? So why act so disgusted with this very direct form of self-injury- so direct that we call it self-injury.

Making them stop isn't the solution-

That one hurts doesn't it? It's so hard to just let it happen. You are not just letting it happen, but demanding they stop this isn't the solution- forcing them to stop isn't the solution. There are problems- real problems that are at the heart of self-injury .You want to find ways to deal with negative emotions that are not so damaging and you also need to help find solutions to the problems. Bad thing is- you may be on your own- there may be no help. Just think about how alone that makes you feel—they feel even more alone in their pain. Just you being there with them helps, though. Not being alone helps them. So- rather than make them stop- **help** them stop—the best and longest that they can.

By the way- do this without conditions and with an honest heart.

SAFE PLACE

To talk- to think- to rest
Give them this- a place where they can explore what's happening and where they can work through some of this out loud and with a little guidance if possible. A place where they can say – I cut myself today because _____and I was feeling this way _____and when I cut myself it made me feel this way _____and then once I was not so highly stressed and I was calmer I felt this way _____and I could have tried some things like this_____Or this_____ and still I made it this long _____ when I was wanting to for this long _____and **I am proud** that I made it longer and through this bad thing, and so I am thinking maybe I can make it longer next time. Maybe discuss other things that might have made it better. Discuss what

led to it- was there a place, a time where it could have been stopped?

Do not drill them or nag them.. best thing is to just let them talk. Don't try to be a counselor—be someone who cares. Let them be safe in knowing that they can talk about this stuff and you still care. Safe that they can explore what is going on inside themselves without judgment or persecution or even an ugly look on your face.

REASONABLE EXPECTATIONS

This is a hard part to take. I know you want fast wonderful results to your efforts, everyone does. It's not going to happen with self-injury.

Every day—every moment without self-injury is a success!

However, every lapse to self-injury isn't a failure. Please get that into your mind and into the mind of whomever you support in this. They will feel like a failure, you may feel like a failure. You know- oh, my gosh- I am doing everything I possibly can and still it isn't enough- still self-injury happens! Well, that's just the way it is. It's not failure – its sort of like in school when you are taking a super hard course—you will have some A days but you will also have some B and C days, and I'm sorry there will be a few D's and F's even- but the course is NOT failed. You just keep going and you keep trying and you just see on average you are successful. Just the fact that you are dealing with it is a major success.

If you are disappointed and feel failure – they will too. Just know- right here- right now—it is most likely going to happen again.. and again. Still there are successful days and you just have to continue.

You know the saying-

you cannot fail unless you quit!

So don't quit and you won't fail! Isn't that encouraging? You cannot fail unless you choose to fail by quitting.

That's all easier said than done and you will feel some really fail-like moments. Deal with them and move forward. And if you say or do the wrong thing- just tell them you're sorry and do better. You are both learning and growing and it's a process that takes time and understanding.

There were many days in the beginning with my daughter where I had been there and done more than I ever thought possible.

Being absolutely supportive and caring without any bad stuff happening. Still she would crash and the only way out she could find - was to cut or burn herself. Sometimes she would tell me but she knew it crushed me so many times she would hide it. Anytime I saw her in long sleeves or a large bracelet on her, I would get a sick feeling. I would wonder if she had slipped, and I would wonder what lies under those covers. Usually I would just let it pass thinking she would talk to me if she wanted to talk. I had a problem bringing it up. I'm not sure why I had a problem just asking, but I did. Maybe I didn't want to confront; maybe I didn't want to invade her space. Maybe I just thought if she did or didn't really wasn't a concern because life today would be the same if she was or wasn't. As time progressed I would ask how she was doing and she would tell me and we would just go on. I don't ask now because it doesn't matter. I know she tries, I know I *will support her and I figure if she wants to talk she will and if she just wants to move forward that's what we are doing.*

So, find a reasonable place to be.
 A place without guilt or blame.
Just reasonable and supportive –when you can be.

The thing is you have to be reasonable with yourself as well. You will have bad days and you will have what you consider failures- you are allowed that. Just don't give up. It will get better and you will both be better stronger closer people for it.

RECOGNIZE

I can't tell you everything to look for but the main thing is you have to be willing to look and willing to accept it is self-injury or you will never see it.

Covering up is a big sign—long sleeves, long pants, lots of bracelets, cuffs, - just abnormally covered. Of course they can injure on their abdomen or other areas that may never be 'uncovered' to you.

Still if you see these changes it is worth considering.

Scratching themselves, punching walls, pulling their own hair, and well, anything that is injury to themselves. It is self-injury.

Hidden stashes of things they can use to injure... their tool-kit. Broken glass, blades

from a razor, hidden knife, burned spoon—
you get the idea—look—be willing to see.

*My first signal of self-injury was when my
daughter got really upset and she dug her
fingernails into her hands. I was upset
enough that I took her to a very high dollar
psychiatrist. He talked to her when she
was eleven and told me she was just a
normal kid. No problem and nothing to
worry about. He gave me nothing to look
for, nothing to read, no warning signs of
things to look for or maybe even some ways
to teach her better coping skills. Just a
clean bill of mental health!*
*It took three years for me to finally see
this on my own—not even knowing what it
was!*

I would say- if you think it is of concern -
then it is—ask them, talk to them and start
working with them as soon as you have a
hint of a thought that they do not know

how to handle bad feelings other than self-injury.

Maybe it is not self-injury per say—but if they can only feel better by hurting themselves then I would say right then is a good time to explore alternative coping skills. Everyone will be different but first sign -- first thought of self-injury--- start trying and searching for alternative coping skills. You don't have to label it to know—if this person is upset and they relieve the upset by injuring themselves then lets find a better way to relieve the negative emotions other than self-injury!

Anyway—you recognize it by being willing to recognize it. So look, talk, think—and you will recognize self-injury.

Talk- Don't attack

You have to be careful; you will find you walk a very scary and fine line. You will want to protect and baby them but when you do that too much it can be as bad for them as anything. I guess the extremes are the bad things. You have to still allow them room to have bad days even though it scares you and you only want to protect them.

I protected- well-I protect my daughter and try very hard to keep her from any harsh moments in life because they can cause a crash. This has lead us to her being very dependent on me and in a way it seems to be very bad for her. She has lost confidence that she can handle life on her own. I have over done it and probably crippled her progress. I am so afraid she will drop back into self-injury that. The harsh things in life- I do my best to block and this keeps her safe from it but also has taken her ability to be on her own accomplishing things this process makes her feel worthless. Then it's hard to get out of this vicious circle. She feels like a loser because she doesn't do things to move forward in life so I baby her and she lets me and she does less so she feels even worse. I still struggle with this and she does too. How do we step beyond her comfort zone.

Anyway- you have to find a way to have open communication. It's really hard. And you really may not understand each other- but you have to understand that you both care and want things to be better. You may have to find creative ways to communicate. The obvious is to speak and listen. Obvious isn't always the easiest.

You might find it easier to send emails so that you can read, absorb, try to understand and when you respond- take your time. With email you can write and rewrite your communication. You can take a break and go back and read it and edit it. This might be a really good place to start so that you have time to edit the communication.

Texting is another option. This one might be a little harder but still instant and without the facial expressions or the eye contact that can be so very intimidating. If you try texting back and forth it can open lines of communication and still allow for some distance. Any step you can take to communicate is a good step.

Letter writing might be an option if it works okay for both parties. Letter writing has become very old school but it is still effective and allows for a more personal touch than texting and emails.

A chalkboard or dry erase board can work for smaller communications as can the bathroom mirror.

Phone calls are good too... and then there is online chatting.

Lots of options to get communication started. I realize you may live in the same house, but it still can work with different forms of communication.

My daughter and I can sit 20 feet apart in the same house and be on Facebook or online, just chatting. We utilize texting like you would never believe. It is amazing how much communication can be achieved by texting. Just some small talk can help to open communication lines. We also email back and forth. We write notes and we use to write quick notes on the bathroom mirror with markers or lipstick.

Whatever works for you- for it- if you don't know what works for you try it until you can get somewhat comfortable with a form of communication – or several forms.

Now—how to communicate
This is the really hard part, I think- How to communicate effectively without attacking each other? This is especially hard if there is guilt and blame present. If you can take those two simple things out of the equation you have accomplished so much.
Even so—you might set some basic guidelines to follow...

You can say how you feel--- but they **do not** make you feel that way.
" So I feel" -----is okay.
" You make me feel" ---- is not okay.

Don't apply pressure for answers or change.
" Will you try to" -this is okay.
" Promise you will" -this is not okay.

Demanding a reason why is not a good thing
" Can you tell me what's going on"- this is okay
" Why are you doing this"-this is not okay.

You need to set personal guidelines, agree to them, and stick to them. If later down the road you find it compelling to overstep any guidelines—you can request a change in guidelines but never push it or demand it.

Your guidelines might be:
For the next 30 days we will follow these guidelines. On mm/dd/yyyy we will discuss and revise our guidelines.

Don't ask to see my cuts
Don't make me feel bad for how you feel
Don't bring up the day when _____
Don't discuss a new counselor

Don't threaten me with being locked away
Don't make me talk about this
Don't use my kitchen knife to cut yourself
Don't make me feel bad for how you feel
Don't bring up the time I _____
Don't shut me out or not talk for more than 1 day
Don't kill yourself
Don't let a wound go without treatment

Sign it, keep it and respect it.

You will know your buttons that set you down a bad path.. make sure – no matter how long the guidelines- that you are comfortable with them and can agree and comply.
Whatever you do-- no matter how bad it gets—do not attack a self-injurer to satisfy your emotional issues. If you cannot help—then step back and get some help for yourself!

handling your issues -on your own

Your problems are not their problems- they have enough to deal with; they do not need to feel like they are tearing you apart. I'm not saying hide your emotions—I am saying you have to handle your emotions. You cannot fall apart on them and lean on them. You can feel free to talk to them like you would about your stuff... bad day at work, problem with friends, not sure if you should dye your hair, feeling fat--- but do not dump your emotional stress from this on them. So if you feel guilty and overwhelmed, then you need to get someone you can get help from. Seek help from a counselor, a friend, anyone that you can talk with freely without compromising your relationship with the self-injurer.

I didn't have much support. I beat myself up and wondered and beat myself up some more and tried to figure out: if I had done something differently, maybe things would have gone better for my daughter. I wondered on things all the way back to her baby times. Finally- I came to terms with the fact that I cannot turn back time so it really didn't matter what I might have done wrong or differently or any of that- at this point we were moving forward and that was all I could change- where we were going - not where we had been. I had to remind myself many times not to dwell on the past and trying to fix it in the past in my mind because it wouldn't help anything. My energy needed to be on the present and the path we were taking. I forced that on myself until it became easy—easier.

Mostly, please remember this is not about you or how it makes you feel. This has to be selfless support of the self-injurer. When you are tired you will have to find a way to rejuvenate – whatever that may be. You may need to tell them you have to go rest for a minute and get their agreement to let you rest and for them not to self injure for that moment. Don't make it a long time. I am talking about two hours or so. Tell them honestly and as reasonably as possible. Don't wait until you are exhausted or worn out or at your ropes end. Don't put additional stress on them.

If you have a support system that is wonderful or if you have other people who can help that is even better.

My son who was only a teen himself was our other support. He handled it good sometimes and other times he would crash a little. He always handled it with love and care for his sister. Maybe that's what matters most. Maybe they need to know you care – you love them unconditionally and you are not giving up or turning away.

Her brother was with her the times I couldn't be. He even worked a night job for a while so that one of us could be there for her at all times. He was amazing and he never faltered on how much he loves her.

Anyway- it is about them not you- not anything about you or your pain or your drama.

Still you can be honest with them about your thoughts and your feelings. Just do it calmly and without blame.

Because,
 your feelings are your responsibilities.

stigma

All other addictions and issues seem to have a sense of understanding and empathy. Self-injury has this stigma—this almost disgust that people give you.
They treat the person like something horrific and awful. They do not understand and most don't try to understand at all. They assume awful things and show little compassion in most cases.
This reaction causes most people to keep it secret and hidden. This amplifies the problem and makes it more difficult for people to get help, support and understanding.
When my daughter went for help people were awful they reacted so horribly that I felt I needed to protect her. It was like she was worse than kids who did drugs, attempted suicide, had eating disorders, smoked, drank or had sex addictions. I still do not understand this. Her brother was so

wise—he told me "aren't you glad its not drugs—if it were drugs her scars would be on her brain—her mind". Yes, I could be thankful for that. But why do counselors seem to be better equipped to empathize with drugs than this? We can only hope that the general public will begin to realize this is real and its not any worse than any other addictive release—if we can reach that point then maybe we can get some help. Maybe they can talk openly without the stigma.

When my daughter was having health problems (a diseased gallbladder) the staff at the hospital would change their behavior towards her when they saw her scars. They knew what it was and you could see the behavior change from compassion and care to near disgust and disdain. Ironically- not one doctor or nurse out of 37 emergency room trips and multiple doctor visits—not one—ever mentioned it to me or tried to give any help for it. It was so bad that the emergency room said she was having mental health issues (still never mentioning the marks on her flesh) and she needed to go to the mental health hospital and she was not physically ill. We went-- and they did ask about the self-injury and they said she needed intensive deep therapy and should be admitted immediately. Thank God I listened to her and trusted her when she said she really was hurting. They said she was faking and only doing it either for attention or anxiety. Three days later when her doctor said it was no way gallbladder and she had a fried chicken sandwich- we rushed back to the emergency room and they removed her diseased gallbladder right away. Had I left her in the mental hospital that said she wasn't really in physical pain... I can only assume her gallbladder would have ruptured and rotted in her body and killed her. Because they never would have listened to her.

Yes, I am angry.

Sometimes I find I am angry because there is so little information and professionals give the wrong advice, and many times I felt they did more harm than good. Mostly the anger boils up when I think about the times I followed their advice and they were wrong – I should have listened to her, but they were so against her because of her scars.

So- we can only hope that the people who suffer from this will step forward and go public and share their pain, their need for help and understanding and maybe then after the public realizes how wide spread this is—maybe then we will get some help and understanding. Then maybe we can find some ways to deal with this. At the very least maybe we can ease the pressure and remove the additional issues caused by people who do not understand.

Schools are a real problem and even child protective services. They make it where you almost have to hide it, or they will accuse the parents of being bad parents. Guess what- many good parents – good homes have these issues—its just very well hidden.

Schools think they are doing well by intervening and usually they only make it worse and child protective services usually is more of a burden on the already stressed situation.

If the stigma can be removed then hopefully the help and understanding will come.

This needs help not more pressure to hide it. They need to be able to seek medical or mental health help without the fear of being taken from their family. There are times when help is needed- it would be nice if it could be sought without adding to the problem.

Removing the stigma of self-injury would allow for open medical help.

medical stuff to share-not scare -

This is part of the really scary stuff---

Necrotizing fasciitis— flesh eating bacteria
Yuck but yes... it could happen. You can
open your flesh and this bacteria can find
its way in and within such a short time can
do irreversible damage and even death.
Using sanitized items for the self-injury
and proper after care of the wounds helps
to avoid this.

Bleeding out—this is an obvious scare and
has to be considered. Consider a no cut
zone around areas that are more apt to
have bloodlines that can easily bleed too
much.

Infection—again obvious but when it's
hidden its harder to care for wounds so

they might go untreated and hidden and become infected and dangerous.

Sad thing is if you go to the doctor and they recognize self-injury they might not empathize and they might report you – if it's your child doing this it could lead to child protective services involvement. Of course if you are just trying to hide self-injury – then it is really hard to explain a dangerous wound you want treatment for especially if you have scars.

Here's where part of the whole stigma thing comes in—a reluctance to seek help when you need it because of the stigma.
It takes a different sort of medical professional to help.
Our family doctor never mentioned it. I'm guessing he knew what it was but didn't have any answers. He never asked anything or told me anything. I never really knew if our pediatrician saw the marks and

understood or if he ignored them. I surely never asked him- I was afraid. I was afraid of the system telling me how to handle this very delicate and personal situation. I figured if he got involved and her school got involved they might take her from me and at the very least demand mind altering medication.

However once she was an adult I wasn't so concerned that she would be taken. Still, when she was ill with her gallbladder and we made 37 trips to the emergency room--- not one medical professional ever said a word.

What if I hadn't known and wasn't supporting her and she was dealing with it all on her own. Why didn't they talk to her or discreetly take me aside and just tell me to look up self-injury. Anyway—it would be really nice if we could get it -where a person can actually – safely- ask for help.

I have hope this day will come- I recall the days when eating disorders and child abuse were hidden due to the reaction a person would get. I believe we can get some help for everyone. We have to start with medical professionals everywhere. They have to know enough to react with compassion and empathy or who will be brave enough in this situation to ask for help?

If you have to go to the doctor and they do address it be prepared that there might be forced hospitalization. You will need to have your child prepared for separate questioning. If they indicate any inclination towards suicide they will be hospitalized. This goes for adults as well. This is where it would come in handy to have a counselor so that you can prove you are seeking help and dealing with it.

It's nearly unbearable to need help and have no way to get it because you know the reaction you will get.

Friends, family, professionals, usually seem to be at a loss to openly discuss self-injury without a look of disgust or confusion.

Honestly from all stand points there is a level of shame being put on all involved. The injurer knows the reaction- all too well, and the person who supports them and tries to find answers feels a certain shame at having let this happen to a loved-one.

It took a while before I was comfortable telling people that my daughter has a problem with self-injury. Usually they really do not react well at all. The best they can offer is silence or a statement acknowledging that they didn't know. I get no understanding, no empathy, and no response on the most part.

I am an extremely strong person so I really do not care what the reaction is- I suspect if I looked for some sort of approval or understanding I would be met with some ugly conversations. When I tell anyone it is very matter of fact, unapologetic, and without concern for his or her response.

I cannot imagine what some people deal with when they only hope for honesty and understanding. I am sure there are some good responses and some really hurtful ones.

Early on—

One 'friend' said it was because I was a single parent and it was against God's plan.

My family member that I had hoped would help pretended like the conversation never happened.

A preacher friend said to pray.

Our doctor avoided the subject.

Her father said it wasn't his fault.

None of these were of any real help.

Those are the worst responses—the best have been - like I said- no response at all.

Be prepared to be met with any number of reactions. Be prepared to be stronger than you ever thought you could.

I know speaking out is scary. As I write this I know many people who know my daughter and me do not know this- it's never come up. Our family doesn't know this openly. My daughter assures me she can handle people knowing. I have stepped into this now. She is here with me and pretty strong. But it's time to say something - someone has to get this out there and then we all have to do something to help.

I have to add- be careful who you tell. Without understanding comes some very dangerous and harmful reactions.

I don't know what causes it and my guess is—
not just one thing, but just a way to
release, to feel—to cry.
Maybe we should start as early as possible
teaching our children ways to handle
extreme emotions. Maybe that would help.

Once self-injury starts- well, we still need
to find other ways to react to situations-
ways other than self-injury.
You cannot just 'not do it'- you have to find
other ways to handle the feelings that lead
to self-injury.

Finding other releases!

There has to be a release- pressure valve-
or really bad things can happen. The best
thing that can happen is to find a
replacement release. If you just 'fight'
doing it, then it will build up and finally it
will have to happen. Finding a release, a
replacement to self-injury is a major step
in dealing with this.
Exercise-
Exercise is the favorite of mine- it's
healthy its beneficial and it releases some
really good stuff into the body that
counteracts the bad stuff happening.

Art is another good release. You can try
every medium- art doesn't have to be
productive or good it just has to happen.
Free-form art is the best way to start just
in case the self critical nature of the self
injurer will lead to more self criticism
about the artwork. Free form art does not

allow for much failure --still, there is clay, making jewelry, splatter paint, paint, welding, and even fixing hair or makeup.

yard work
video games
karate
dance
yoga
singing
jogging
cleaning
remodeling
music
pets
reading
writing
interaction with others
biking
walking dog
treadmill
ironing
folding towels
scanning pictures

internet research

baking

swimming

Violent video games—yes, that's right... it's a good release for anger- it's safe and it doesn't hurt anyone.

PUPPIES- puppies make everything better- but they do grow into dogs... still pets help us so much!

"Many self-injurers like myself have enormous amounts of rage within and are sometimes afraid to express it outwardly, we injure ourselves as a way of venting these feelings without hurting others. When intense feelings built, I became overwhelmed and unable to deal with it. By causing pain, I could reduce the level of emotional stress to a bearable one. As a teenager it was an escape from the numbness many of those who self-injure say they do it in order to feel something, to know that they're still alive. You obtain a certain feeling of euphoria. Continuing abusive patterns later in life became more force of habit an adrenal rush on stage rather then a cry for help." Daughter's note 2011

Professional help and drugs

I don't know what to say here except I hope professionals will learn to deal with this with compassion and understanding.

I don't know how to tell you to get help from a professional because we never were able to find anyone who was of help.

I started to end this section right here—with a giant ---- Good Luck!

Yes, I have animosity towards psychiatrist, and psychologists—and counselors. They all failed us and yes we quit trying with them. But we quit because it was such a horrific let down when they basically threw their hands up.

It's new for them and they are human and just like most people this is hard to deal with for them.

Still I give them no compassion no empathy and no understanding. They are supposed to be able to help and rather than try to

find answers and solutions that work they-
well- they didn't.

When you cannot find any professional that
can help you- and when you try one after
the other it makes you feel like it's
hopeless and you are hopeless and well it's
the icing on the cake of feeling alone and
help-less!
Self-injury is real and yet it doesn't seem
to be popular with the professional help
people! They want to find answers in other
mental health issues. The ones who try
usually try to help with what they know
from other things. There seems to be very
little attempt to understand and therefore
really help with self-injury. *I apologize to
the professionals out there I am lumping in
with this general rant against them. I am
sure there are some out there who help. I
have met only two that were not disgusted
and one of those was two busy with their
own issues to help and the other may have*

just come along too late. We had been through so much and insurance benefits were no longer in place so my daughter felt obligated to get better faster which wasn't helping the process. Still, 8 years into it we did meet one reasonable and considerate counselor. My daughter has maintained friendly contact with him and he did offer some amazing insight into our relationship. Out of many I can say I appreciate one professional who met this issue with respect, intelligence and care.

This is real and it affects so many people, but it is hidden and shunned. If mental health professionals would get on this and learn about it and work with it and find some answers and some fixes... but mostly some compassion and empathy then maybe they could help lead others to a better place and then with the stigma gone- then maybe there would be help!

It's like several years ago we didn't know what eating disorders were- and until it killed a famous singer we never heard of it. Even after that it took several years to find empathy and understanding. And finally years later we are at least at place socially that we can help rather than hide, ridicule and shun.

The thing is- self-injury doesn't ever have to kill- it can be hidden and covered up and possibly never addressed. It's a real problem for so many more people than you realize. I promise you it is not isolated to any group. They need help and the people who love them need help and the mental health professionals are not getting it. Again – sorry for the animosity- but I think it is their responsibility and they are failing at it- at us. And because they won't even see it- well, why should anyone else?

This needs to be discussed, addressed and there needs to be some compassion and empathy put in place – right now.

I started with an actual psychiatrist. I figured we should start with the best. Immediately when we went for our first session—without discussion or exam or blood-work or anything—immediately they said my 14-year-old daughter needed to be on anti-depressants. We were very much against any drugs in our home and that was the way my children were raised. My daughter deeply wanted to control this without drugs. The psychiatrist gave her a list of ten drugs to choose from- sent her home to research them. She did and found that not one had any research on anyone under 18! None of them were tested on minors, but they are heavily prescribed to them. Even worse, every one of the drugs he recommended listed suicide as a possible side effect. It was bad enough that my daughter was cutting herself, I surely didn't want to put her on a medication that had SUICIDE listed as a possible side effect! She told him this on our next visit and she said she wasn't taking anything that wasn't proven to be safe for her age group. I was proud of her decision, but I knew our road would be even harder—it would be easier, I am sure, to drug someone rather than deal with the issues at hand. I knew she would have a hard battle ahead and I was sure I would do anything I could to help her. The hardest thing we learned in that meeting was how insistent these doctors are about medicating the problem. When we made the decision to try this battle without drugs the psychiatrist appeared to be done with us! When we told him "no, we don't want to medicate." He made it clear that if we were truly invested in her well-being and recovery we would agree to antidepressants. She told him she wanted help but she wanted to resolve these problems without drugs. He made it absolutely clear to us that refusing drugs - was, in his opinion refusing help. So- what I learned in that first visit was—if you do not do what the professional help dictates to you—then they label you 'uncooperative' and pretty much write you off. So if you say, "no, we don't want to take drugs" – or drugs labeled "side-effects include suicide!" – Then you are not cooperating and therefore deserve no help—that's what you hear- but I think it is more simply- they don't know what to do besides drug you—they don't know how to help- so rather than say they don't understand and there's too little research and they just don't know how to help—they say – well, you are not taking the drugs I suggested so you are not even wanting help and I'm not wasting time on this. If medication is the route a family chooses then that is fine, but options should be available. We went through one counselor after another from every level of expertise. It's a very expensive thing to do-- even with good insurance and if you don't have good insurance I don't know— guess you better be rich.

But you have to pay to speak to them and you should give them a chance to build a working relationship... and it's a meeting a week or so—so it's a waste of money and time very often. I am sorry to say that but it was—I tried talking to them and screening them. They all said they could help and they understood self-injury. They didn't understand, and I would tell them she was not quick to share her feelings so they would need to build a relationship with her before getting into the self-injury and that we did not want to medicate.

It was like I never said this--- and once we absolutely refused drugs the doctor sent us to someone else, 'who might be able to help us under our chosen circumstances'. This meant immediately downgrading to a counselor!

So- Counselor #1 was a reasonable, very nice and respectable looking young woman, she looked to be a recent graduate and I hoped she might have some current education that made her aware of self injury. She was brought up to date on basics by the psychiatrist. We met with her and I could see it all over her face-- she was appalled at this behavior! She had dealt with drug abuse, suicide attempts, and aggressive traits in teens, but never self-injury, and it was all over her face—this grimace of disgust. I only hoped my daughter didn't see it or that I was imagining it. The three of us met and I explained my daughter is a little shy with strangers and obviously not comfortable talking about self injury. I explained we were fine with whatever time it took to build a relationship where my daughter would feel comfortable discussing her personal issues and then working towards a resolution. She agreed that 'of course' this is delicate and we will take our time working into such delicate issues. We were fine with the time and expense but wanted the steps to be comfortable. She agreed with our plan and then asked if we were comfortable with her speaking to my daughter alone. My daughter goes in to talk to her and is out in 10 minutes. This 'professional at dealing with teenagers' straight out asked my daughter 'why are you doing this?' my daughter answered she didn't know and the woman insisted that she must know why she does this. She told my daughter she would have to tell her if she wanted help. Then my daughter clammed up, that's just what she did back then when she was stressed out and met with force. She wasn't being rude she just didn't know what to say. Then of all things- this woman said "well, if you don't want to talk, that's your choice -I get paid if we talk or not- so we can just sit her in silence for an hour'. My daughter got up, came to the waiting room and told me what was said – the counselor followed her out, heard what she said, and never denied a word-she only said she was trying to get her to talk. We left and never returned to that office. We left there and I felt beat, my daughter however felt a huge mass of awful feelings. We talked on the drive home. I think this is the best thing you can do—just talk. Not lecture- not question.. Just honest, open dialogue. That in itself is a little hard to learn but it's worth it. She told me that she felt awful at hurting my feelings and her brother's and that she really just didn't know why she felt compelled to do it. Well that was just one counselor and I assured her we would just keep trying. We tried several times to find the right counselor.

Each time is harder to face and harder to be hopeful about getting any help.

Counselor #2 was a man casual and reasonable and older... I hoped maybe a father figure. We went to his office and had the same basic conversation where I asked for him to work with her and give her time to get comfortable and he agreed and assured me he always does this. We talked and he told me I needed to be prepared because often there are repressed memories of sexual assault that cause self-injury. I doubted it but told him I understood- we would deal with whatever we need to deal with. So the three of us talked a moment- my daughter was sort of quiet as usual. Then Counselor #2 asked if he could speak with her alone. My daughter was okay with it so I stepped into the lobby. After about 30 minutes he called me into his office. He told me she seemed okay besides the self-injury and that there wasn't a lot he could help with beyond medication. Wow! Okay, no problems beyond self-injury! Thank you? I didn't ask my daughter what was said, but she told me. He started off the conversation with --- has anyone sexually abused you? And – Are you bisexual? Really? That's easing into a relationship? She told me she really didn't think she was sexually abused and she told him she didn't know what her sexual preference was- that she was only 14. So that was our big help from Counselor #2.

Another one-
I called and talked to her on the phone and she said my daughter was sexually abused that is what this stems from and I needed to be ready to face this. She said this without talking to my daughter. And she went on to say if we didn't want to medicate she couldn't help us. She said we had to be willing to follow treatment.

Another one-

I went to speak with her and she had the most appalled look on her face so I left and never subjected my daughter to her.

Another one-

Immediately asks - 'are you getting the attention you want?' So we left shortly thereafter. Since my daughter was initially hiding it and I made that clear- why would a counselor even think this?

 Another counselor- *this one was a lovely, practically insane woman....*
We talked awhile as a group and she seemed like she might be helpful. I was even okay that the way she was building a relationship was talking about what animal would you be if you could be any animal and went on talking about what animal she would be—

There were more sessions with varying degrees of unusual but at least open dialogue.

She did try to build a relationship without pressure...however she went on vacation every other week so there was no way to build a comfortable relationship.

I picked my daughter up from school for another session and she said she didn't want to try the counseling any more. She said it was stressing her out more and making her feel more like self-injuring. She said she would prefer we handle it.

So my daughter told me the counselors made it worse and made her feel more stress and asked if we could just work on it together. I knew this, I saw this – she was right, she realized before I did- that there was no help. I agreed to try anything she wanted to try.

I understood what she meant there is such a build up of anticipation and hope before each session. All the searching and talking and then there is no help or they ask stupid questions.   It all had to be sexual orientation or sexual abuse or something that could only be controlled with drugs. And the intensity that each one of these sessions created was horrible for all of us and then to have no results no hope and no help.

So we tried counseling for about six months and then we were on our own as a family.

Counselors do not have enough information to help- not the mass of them- so if there are any who actually help... they are not easily located.

I forgot the school counselors --if we should even count those people. Why do they call them counselors? Most are not credentialed counselors.

School counselors---

My apologies for being so up front and rude, but these people are not equipped to deal with real issues and should not try. *We included my daughter's counselor in the issues we were facing. She did try to understand- she read some information I gave her, but there was very little. Her help was hurting. The counselor was just one more problem. We asked if my daughter could go to the school for kids with problems. This was usually for teens that were pregnant or had gotten into legal trouble. It was a self-paced school with smaller groups. You had to apply- long story short—they said she couldn't attend. Still my daughter's counselor was better than some.* Some school counselors I have heard of reporting the parents to child protective services and adding more pressure to an already extreme situation. It's no help. Its not understood and they insist on counseling that rarely helps. So they end up putting the family through so much more- when they are already dealing with all they can handle. We need some information out there so that school counselors can help rather than make it worse. And 'child protective services' needs to understand this better as well. I will say the people I know who have had CPS called on them—once CPS investigates they tell the school counselor to back off. Still I have known people who pull their kids out of school because the counselor puts their kid through so much more than they are already dealing with at the time.

What is the requirement to be a school counselor? I am pretty sure they are not real counselors- so they need to either learn more or be reasonable and understanding. That being said I am sure there is the occasional school counselor who is reasonable and helpful. To those – I thank you. To the others who think they are helping when they know so little- please realize how much damage you can do- and please just stop.

Religious help

I am sure there is help in faith and I am sure it works for some people.

So a friend of mine suggested my daughter go to a revival in town and it was all kids her age. She wouldn't go alone, so I called a relative who we had helped many times and asked if she would go with her. She was a young adult in the right age group and very involved in church and religion. I asked if she could help, if my family would help. The response was she had to babysit for another family member. I never asked for help of any kind for my entire adult life. When we asked for help from my strong Christian family-They said no. I was sitting in my car in a parking lot when my family said "no, they couldn't help, but for me to pray". Sorry, that was not helpful. I guess the saying is 'just because you pray for something and you don't get it doesn't mean God isn't listening—it just means he said 'no". Okay, fair enough—at least when you know there is no help – you know what to expect. There I sat knowing it was all whatever the three of us could manage- without help from anyone. I guess some will say that was the help.... Okay. And the thing that God never gives you more than you can handle. Okay. Its ten years and yes, we have handled it. So I won't argue these points. And maybe there is a divine plan. Maybe it is to help others. I'm okay with that. Not crazy of what my daughter has had to endure, but yes she is strong and yes, our family is strong. So we can go with that- if only this does help someone somewhere. Well, to me, her mom, her pain is not worth it, but she is much nicer than I am. So maybe she would be okay with her suffering- helping others. And I know anyone who prays and believes, prefers it to be a positive good thing.

So, okay God had a plan? Okay.

Still my family chose babysitting (anyone of them could have babysat the kids) over helping my daughter—so no, I don't believe they were in on the plan. They left us sitting there with no help. All the talks of leading others to God—and here was a chance and they didn't even try. That was it as far as asking anything from them ever again.

The few preachers I talked to really didn't have a clue about it and seemed scared of it. I respect that- at least they did not say they could help and didn't have a clue how to help. They offered prayer, and suggested professional help. I respect that.

So we were left with-
My daughter, her brother and me.

And we all love each other so much—did then and still do. It was just something to get through, but without help.

Wondering 'why'-is a waste- its here- deal with it

That was hard to get through—my mind always racing around -where did I mess up—what could I have done differently—if I could go back in time where would it be— over and over and more and more---

But you know what? We cannot change the past so we move forward. That's all I can tell you on that.
Wondering and searching for the answer is a waste of valuable resources. It's here so you deal with it.

We can work with that.
I don't have that 'why' answer for anyone. Guess it might help others to know that, but the self-injury victims seem to come from every walk of life with various circumstances.

If you are dealing with it - just deal with it--- maybe someday there will be an answer to why...

I even tried to blame braces—maybe the metal.
Maybe her baby food, or water we drank or maybe the fact that I lectured against drugs and alcohol and bad behavior but never once considered self-injury. Maybe everyone has to have a release for their stress and strain and maybe my generation knew to beat it in our kids' heads to stay away from all this bad stuff—so it has to be released somehow... so here is self-injury? That's sort of the only answer I can come up with. You would be surprised how many people resort to self-injury.

We have been dealing with it for 10 years now—
I am amazed that there is still so little help.

Their need for privacy~

That's hard to swallow- I know you want to snoop and investigate. You think if you have more information you can do something to fix it.   You wonder if maybe whatever information you might find -maybe its life saving.   *I wanted to look through my daughter's writings and her email and her social media but I promised her privacy.* They have to have a place to freely release their thoughts. If you can truly give this to them, then offer it up. But do not breech the trust. In return, you can explain that you need to know if they are suicidal or maybe hiding an injury that won't heal. Or if there is any thought or feeling you can help with to please tell you.   They are already dealing with so much we just don't understand and they need every possible release. So if they can write it down and get it on paper then maybe it will help.

They have to be able to do this freely. So you have to give them some privacy.

It won't do you any good to sneak a peek. You have to just absolutely leave it alone. It's hard but if they can trust you, on this, then they will gain the ability to trust you more and build on this. Ideally they will talk to you, but even so they need a place for thoughts to flow without hesitation or fear. Give this to them. It's hard sometimes because you think you will find answers. But please just let them have a little private place to release their confused thoughts.

Get past making it about your relationship...

I spent way too many hours making it about us—it was about my daughter and how she handles things---- just because she has an issue and it leads to self-injury doesn't mean it's about us or what is going on or what I did or didn't do...

DO you understand what I am saying? While they need help and support and love and the best understanding you can offer- they still get to have ownership of this issue. So when it happens- don't fall apart, don't go through the whole blame process. It's a true waste of time and there's no need for it. It really isn't going to help anyone or anything. Now this is assuming there are no external forces pushing anxiety and pressure onto your self-injurer.

External forces at work

If you have external forces in your world that are adding anxiety and pressure to the situation- do your best to remove it—or help the person who is suffering from self-injury remove any unnecessary pressures.

So – if you have an abuser in the house you need to try to stop that problem.

Abuse is not always physical- emotional, mental and sexual abuse shouldn't be in any home, but definitely not in the home of someone already suffering from self-injury issues.

Extreme pressures for grades or performance might be lessened.

Fighting and arguing should be kept to a minimum.

Parental discord should not fall on a child.

If there are external forces under the control of the self-injurer only- then try to help them realize and find ways to alleviate these problems.

These types of issues will only cause more stress and more anxiety. If you can stop or ease any of these negative situations then do it. I would say do it with the agreement of the person suffering from self-injury. Don't use this as an excuse to force your opinion on them.

When my daughter started self-injury I did the normal parent thing—well, one of them. I tried blaming her music. She was listening to some really dark disturbing music at times. Of course other times it was classical and even other times it was some really upbeat stuff. Still I tried to believe it had to do with the dark music. This made her angry at me because it made no sense to her. And looking back I get it— she was listening to the music in response to her feelings not the other way around. Fortunately I only asked if it was the music causing these moods. She responded that it wasn't and went on to explain her different musical preferences. It made sense and I let it go. It would have been so nice if it had been her music and the simple answer would be to get rid of that music... but that wasn't the problem... the problem wasn't her friends or what she watched on television or video games. That would have been so easy—but it was something inside of her that she was dealing with. There was no getting rid of the problem easily. It takes time and work and some really bad moments.

Risk of making them too dependent

As if there's not enough to worry about you also have to worry about making them too dependent. I didn't know what to do when all this started, I really still don't know what to do. The only thing I can figure out was to protect my daughter at all costs. To be there for her any time she needed me, if at all possible. To help her cope with her issues, to talk to her when she wanted to talk, to keep as much pressure off of her as I possibly could, in short to do anything and everything I possibly could to keep her away from self-injury. You know we've been at it over 10 years, now and it's still a struggle.

Still we are all good and she does better every day. It's been over a year, maybe close to two years. I am so proud of her for accomplishing so much without much help or understanding.

They still have to handle their emotions on their own... so when we cradle them it has dangers as well.

Today my daughter- who has been dealing with self-injury for over a decade of her 25 years had her sleeves pulled up... her gorgeous beautiful arms have scars from her wrists to her elbows. Scars from cuts on the outer arm and burn scars on the inner arms. Her shoulders have scars from burns. There are a more that I don't often see. It hurts to see the scars, but at one time she let me know the scars mean something important to her. They are marks of suffering she has survived. I don't fully understand and it hurts to see them, but I guess I get it. She hurt so bad she did this and maybe seeing it helps her through it all.
I cannot say I fully understand or that I even expect that I will. I do know I love her unconditionally and completely. I know

she has handled so much without help. I know I am proud of the strength she shows with getting through this unknown problem without help. And I know there are so many others out there that suffer quietly and still without help. It's a dark, very well kept secret of many people. I don't know what it will take to get help. But it's not a rare problem. It's as real and wide spread as eating disorders. If we can somehow get past the fear and anxieties we suffer as a society, at knowing about it and find a way to help. Then maybe we can see progress and an end to something that shouldn't be left in hiding.

This is real and it's hard to deal with and rather than make it harder we need to get some help for everyone who is working through this – or hiding it.

self-criticism-
they don't need help with that

It seems that would be self-explanatory. It also seems that if you have a person in your life that already suffering you wouldn't want to add to it. It's just such an emotional situation. The people that I know that self injure seem to be perfectionists who already criticize themselves more than enough. So before you add to their list of things they're dealing with -- take a deep breath and know they've probably already attacked themselves with the very same thought.

This week my daughter and I are trying to figure out a way to pull back from her perfectionism. I guess that sounds strange to some of you, I guess a lot of people strive for perfection. My daughter and a lot of the people that I met that self injure already suffer at the hands of self-criticism and the desire for perfection.

Constructive self-criticism is a good thing, it helps us do better. But an unreal expectation of perfection and the self-criticism that follows is not healthy at all. If you can find a way to help them ease up on the self-criticism and the perfectionism rather than add to it you will help them get past one of the issues.

Support for the supporter

Some people have more strength and support and ability to get through things. Some people can only take so much and they break. If you are the person who is supporting a self-injurer then you cannot fall apart, you cannot break down and you cannot give up. You may need to find a support system to get you through- Maybe family, maybe church, maybe friends— maybe you can get a support group going. Your support may change from time to time. Whatever you have to do to get through this- just find a way. Support may come from some unexpected places. Since I have been dealing with this I have had other parents come to me for help. I cannot give them a lot, but I do give them understanding and some hope. Maybe help can be found in established addiction support groups. You may learn that the only support you can find will come from new sources. You may learn that your old friends, your family, and even your old counselor cannot help you through this and if that is the case then you need to find new support. It's out there- even if you have to get what help and support you can, and then move on to the next source. You have to have enough strength to help them through whatever it is they have to face.

I made my life about her for over ten years. I felt bad if I even felt happy but that was no help to her. I learned I needed to find some happiness so that I could help her. It's not easy- you feel like you have to focus and be ready for what comes next and any relationships or anything for yourself seems like too much responsibility and frivolous. Still you can find a balance if you communicate with people in your life. Some will understand and can actually help while others will go on their way. Don't isolate yourself because you both need more than your time circle if you are able to find it.

Who does it?

Now, here it would be nice if there were a set formula of who is likely and who is not. Well, I'm sorry to tell you- it's widespread, it's hidden and it's bigger than you think.

People with 'perfect' lives self-injure, people with problems do it, and just your average person does this.

Here's a thought for consideration:

Isn't alcoholism, drug addiction, sex addiction, fighting, punching walls, overeating, eating disorders, and multiple other accepted and treated mental health issues--- aren't they self- injury?

Yes, they are.

These things injure you—it's self injury!

So, really –

who do you know that is a self-injurer?

Maybe a better question is:

who do you know that has never been guilty of some form of self-injury?

The veil needs to be lifted and we need to
deal with this-
it's time.

Maybe it's "Self Injury Disorder"-
maybe changing the name is all it would take
to get some help?

So here I am at the end – time to name this
book--- and there it is—my barely there
conclusion—
Self Injury Disorder, a very clinical
problem.

Now–can we get a little help over here?

still a work in progress

I wish every one of you all the best.
Just one moment at a time get through it...
It really is worth it...

Susan is not a professional in the medical or
mental health fields.
Please read with an open heart and make
your own good decisions.

www.ingramcontent.com/pod-product-compliance
Lightning Source LLC
Chambersburg PA
CBHW070358290526
45790CB00004B/1551